PIANO · VOCAL · GUITAR

THE SONGS OF IRVING BERLIN
BALLADS

CONTENTS

Cover Photo: A formal studio photograph of Irving Berlin taken from the mid-1930's.

ISBN 0-7935-0378-7

Hal Leonard Publishing Corporation
7777 West Bluemound Road P.O. Box 13819 Milwaukee, WI 53213

ALL ALONE

Words and Music by
IRVING BERLIN

Moderate Waltz

Just like a mel - o - dy that lin - gers on,
Just for a mo - ment you were mine, and then

3

all a - lone _____ feel - ing blue, _____

won - d'ring where you are, _____ and how you are _____

and if you are, all a - lone

1. too.

2. too. _____

ALL BY MYSELF

Words and Music by
IRVING BERLIN

ALL OF MY LIFE

Words and Music by
IRVING BERLIN

ALWAYS

Words and Music by
IRVING BERLIN

now that I've found you at last, _____
then that will I my found love lin - ger on. _____

I'll be lov - ing you, al - ways _____

with a love that's true,

al - ways _____ When the things you've

there, al - ways,

not for just an hour, not for just a

day, not for just a year, but al - ways.

al - ways.

BLUE SKIES

Words and Music by
IRVING BERLIN

BECAUSE I LOVE YOU

Words and Music by
IRVING BERLIN

GET THEE BEHIND ME, SATAN

Words and Music by
IRVING BERLIN

THE GIRL THAT I MARRY

Words and Music by
IRVING BERLIN

HOW ABOUT ME?

Words and Music by
IRVING BERLIN

Eb/F F9 F7 Abmaj7/Bb Bb7 Fm/C Bb7/D Eb
when you have for - got - ten. And may - be
R.H.
Ebm6 Bb/D Gm7b5 C7#5 C7
a ba - by will climb up - on your knee and
R.H.
R.H.
Fm Fm7b5 Gm/Bb Bb7
1 Eb6 Gbdim7
put it's arms a - bout you. But how a - bout me?
Fm7 Bb7
2 Eb6 Fm7/Eb Eb6/9
me?
rall.

HOW DEEP IS THE OCEAN
(HOW HIGH IS THE SKY)

Words and Music by
IRVING BERLIN

I CAN'T REMEMBER

Words and Music by
IRVING BERLIN

I GOT LOST IN HIS ARMS

Words and Music by
IRVING BERLIN

I NEVER HAD A CHANCE

Words and Music by
IRVING BERLIN

54

I'M BEGINNING TO MISS YOU

Words and Music by
IRVING BERLIN

IT'S A LOVELY DAY TOMORROW

Words and Music by
IRVING BERLIN

I'M PLAYING WITH FIRE

Words and Music by
IRVING BERLIN

I've heard a-bout you,

MAYBE IT'S BECAUSE
I LOVE YOU TOO MUCH

Words and Music by
IRVING BERLIN

REACHING FOR THE MOON

Words and Music by
IRVING BERLIN

A pale new moon, a sky of

REMEMBER

Words and Music by
IRVING BERLIN

ROSES OF YESTERDAY

Words and Music by
IRVING BERLIN

Slowly

Ros - es of yes - ter - day, _____ fad - ed and

thrown a - way. _____ Love is a pale bou - quet _____

_____ of yes - ter - day's ros - es. _____ Ros - es were once in bloom _____

THE SONG IS ENDED
(BUT THE MELODY LINGERS ON)

Words and Music by
IRVING BERLIN

My thoughts go back to a heav- en- ly dance, a mo- ment of bliss we spent. _____ Our hearts were filled with a song of ro- mance, as

SAY IT ISN'T SO

Words and Music by
IRVING BERLIN

WHEN I LEAVE THE WORLD BEHIND

Words and Music by
IRVING BERLIN

to leave when I grow old, some-how it passed me by.

I'm ver - y poor, but still I'll leave a pre-cious will when I must say good -

bye. _____ I'll leave the sun - shine to the flow - ers, _____ I'll leave the

spring-time to the trees. And to the old folks ___ I'll leave the mem-'ries of a

THEY SAY IT'S WONDERFUL

Words and Music by
IRVING BERLIN

WHAT'LL I DO?

Words and Music by
IRVING BERLIN

WHEN I LOST YOU

Words and Music by
IRVING BERLIN